Green Anacondas

by Grace Hansen

Abdo
SUPER SPECIES
Kids

abdopublishing.com

Published by Abdo Kids, a division of ABDO, PO Box 398166, Minneapolis, Minnesota 55439.

Copyright © 2017 by Abdo Consulting Group, Inc. International copyrights reserved in all countries.
No part of this book may be reproduced in any form without written permission from the publisher.

Printed in the United States of America, North Mankato, Minnesota.

052016

092016

 THIS BOOK CONTAINS
RECYCLED MATERIALS

Photo Credits: iStock, Minden Pictures, Science Source, Shutterstock, SuperStock,
©Ed George p.5/National Geographic Creative ©Vadim Petrakov p.9/ Shutterstock.com

Production Contributors: Teddy Borth, Jennie Forsberg, Grace Hansen

Design Contributors: Laura Mitchell, Dorothy Toth

Cataloging-in-Publication Data

Names: Hansen, Grace, author.

Title: Green anacondas / by Grace Hansen.

Description: Minneapolis, MN : Abdo Kids, [2017] | Series: Super species |
    Includes bibliographical references and index.

Identifiers: LCCN 2015959225 | ISBN 9781680805468 (lib. bdg.) |
    ISBN 9781680806021 (ebook) | ISBN 9781680806588 (Read-to-me ebook)

Subjects: LÇSH: Anaconda--Juvenile literature.

Classification: DDC 597.96--dc23

LC record available at http://lccn.loc.gov/2015959225

Table of Contents

Super Snakes!

Green anacondas are the heaviest snakes in the world. Pythons are often longer. But green anacondas still weigh two times more!

4

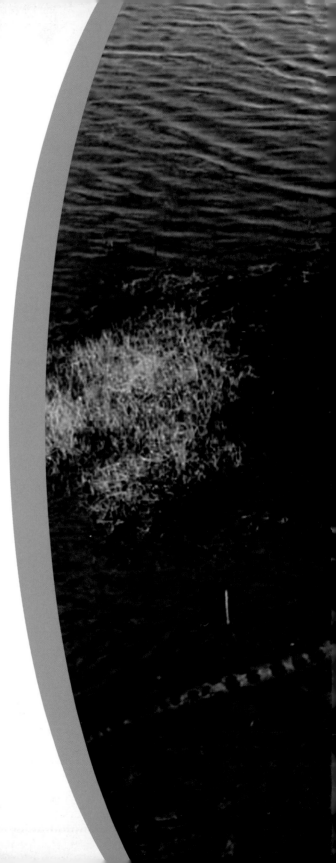

5

Green anacondas can weigh

up to 500 pounds (227 kg).

That is more than a male lion!

7

Green anacondas can grow more than 29 feet (8.8 m) long. A school bus is 45 feet (13.7 m) long.

Green anacondas are **thick**. They can be as big around as an adult human!

Big Eaters

Green anacondas spend most of their time hunting. They have big **appetites**. They eat lots of fish and large **rodents**. They even eat turtles and jaguars!

13

Green anacondas do not poison their prey. They are constrictors. This means, they squeeze prey until it dies.

Green anacondas eat their meals whole. Their jaws stretch apart. They can open their mouths very wide!

After a big meal, the snake can go weeks without eating. It uses this time to rest and **digest**.

Babies

Females give birth to up to 36 snakes. Babies measure one to two feet (.3 to .6 m) in length.